D0407474

Also by the authors

ZooBorns: The Newest, Cutest Animals from the World's Zoos and Aquariums

ZooBorns! Zoo Babies from Around the World

ZooBorns

CATS!

THE NEWEST, CUTEST KITTENS AND CUBS
FROM THE WORLD'S ZOOS

Andrew Bleiman and Chris Eastland

SIMON & SCHUSTER
New York   London   Toronto   Sydney   New Delhi

Simon & Schuster
1230 Avenue of the Americas
New York, NY 10020

Copyright © 2011 by Zooborns LLC

All rights reserved, including the right to reproduce this book or
portions thereof in any form whatsoever. For information address
Simon & Schuster Subsidiary Rights Department,
1230 Avenue of the Americas, New York, NY 10020

First Simon & Schuster hardcover edition November 2011

SIMON & SCHUSTER and colophon are registered trademarks of
Simon & Schuster, Inc.

For information about special discounts for bulk purchases,
please contact Simon & Schuster Special Sales at
1-866-506-1949 or business@simonandschuster.com.

The Simon & Schuster Speakers Bureau can bring authors
to your live event. For more information or to book an event,
contact the Simon & Schuster Speakers Bureau at
1-866-248-3049 or visit our website at www.simonspeakers.com.

Manufactured in the United States of America

10 9 8 7 6 5 4 3 2 1

Library of Congress Control Number: 2011934001

ISBN 978-1-4516-5190-4
ISBN 978-1-4516-5189-8 (ebook)

Thank you to Julia Chosy, Ph.D. Without her dedication, knowledge, and expertise, this book would have far fewer whiskers.

A special thank you to the feline friends in our lives: Ronald, Fluffy, Rotten Ralph, Doofus, the Lulus, Laika and Georgie.

ZooBorns
CATS!

Introduction

When we envision wild felines, we picture lions, tigers, and cheetahs. But did you know that there are thirty-six different species of wild cat, from the tiny black-footed cat and the water-loving fishing cat to the critically endangered Amur leopard? Little is known about many of these cats, but most face conservation challenges from habitat destruction, human encroachment, and even poaching.

Zoos and other international organizations are leading feline conservation efforts, which often include breeding programs. In this book we share many of these kittens, representing the largest number of juvenile feline photos from different species ever assembled in one publication.

Shy and elusive, many of these cats live side by side with human populations that do not even realize they are there. With *ZooBorns Cats!* we hope to bring attention to these rarely seen felines and inspire you, the reader, to do your part to help protect them.

So remember, these adorable cubs are more than just cute, furry faces; they are ambassadors for their seldom seen and increasingly rare wild cousins. Support your local accredited zoo and related conservation programs to ensure the future of these extraordinary felines.

Felid Taxonomic Advisory Group

Association of Zoos and Aquariums

The Association of Zoos and Aquariums sets high standards to make sure all animals at accredited zoos and aquariums get the very best care.

A portion of all proceeds from ZooBorns book sales goes directly to the AZA's Conservation Endowment Fund.

Species: Leopard (Persian)

Names: Chapu & Darius

Home: Zoo Madrid, Spain (Chapu)
ZooParc de Beauval, France (Darius)

Born: 5/1/2009
ZooParc de Beauval, France

Status: Endangered

© Lifeonwhite.com

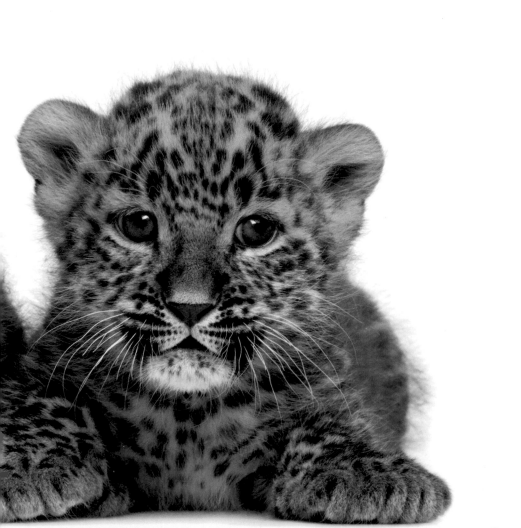

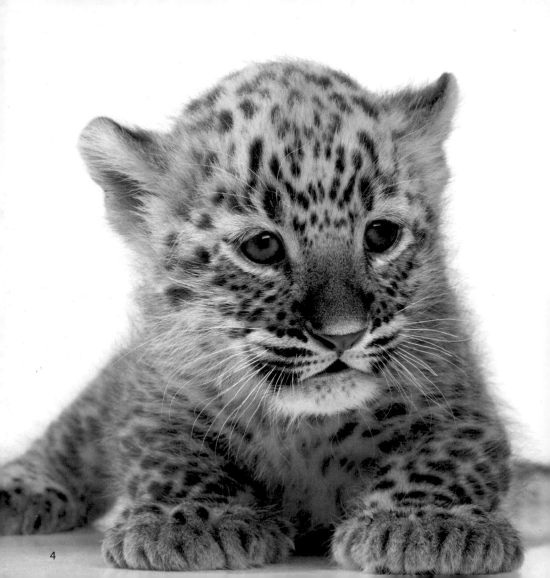

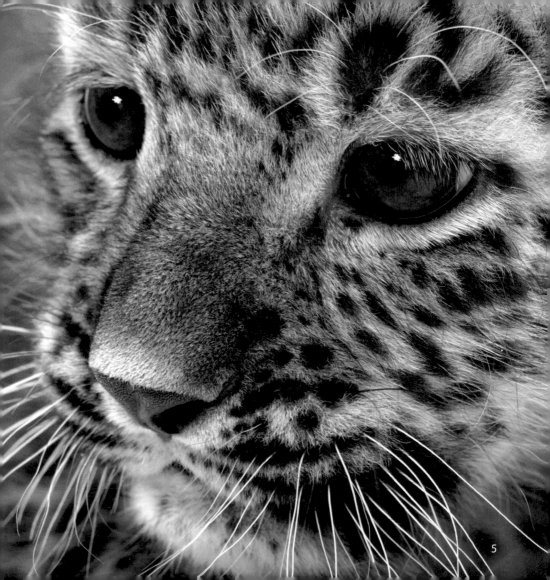

The largest of all leopard subspecies, this majestic feline can reach 130 lbs and measure seven feet long from nose to tail. Roaming forests, grasslands, and mountains, Persian leopards hunt deer, gazelle, goats, and wild boar—occasionally coming into conflict with herders.

Also called the Caucasian leopard, this species inhabits pockets of wilderness throughout Central Asia and the Middle East. Following the collapse of the Soviet Union, poaching of leopards and their prey increased dramatically. Persian leopards are now endangered throughout their range.

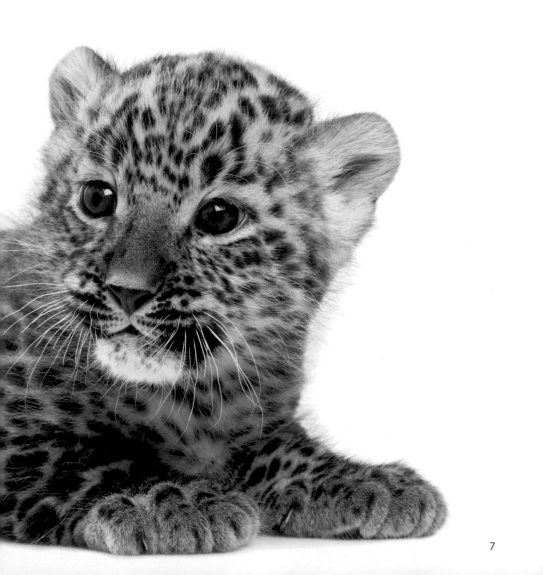

Species: Black-footed Cat

Names: Ali and Abby

Home: Utah's Hogle Zoo, UT (Ali)
Fresno Chaffee Zoo, CA (Abby)

Born: 7/15/2007
Kansas City Zoological Park, MO

Status: Vulnerable

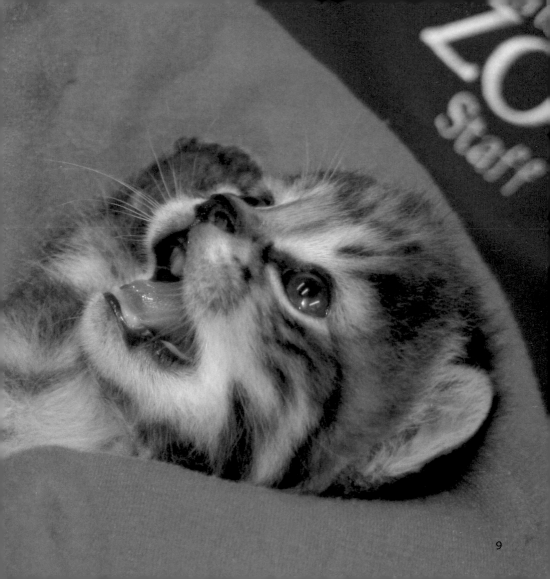

9

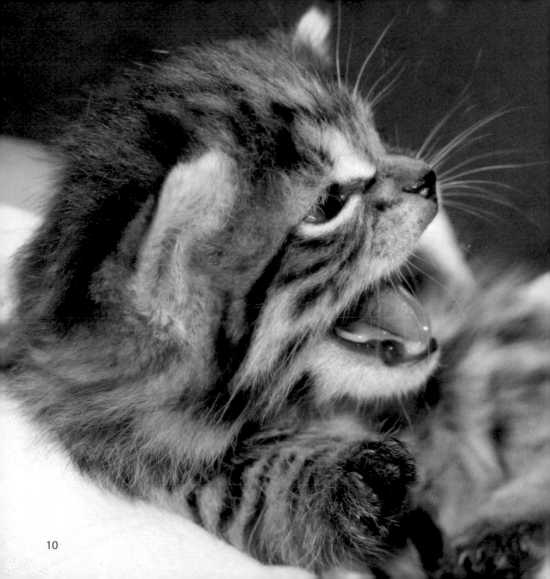

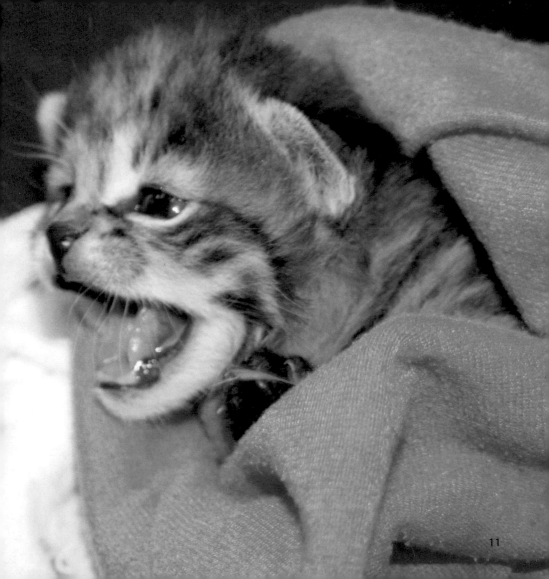

Kansas City Zoo's Director of Conservation Liz Harmon learned first-hand about the cats' habits as she crawled into burrows to learn more about this vulnerable species. Her travels to Africa on behalf of the Black-footed Cat Working Group were key to the development of black-footed cat conservation programs within accredited zoos.

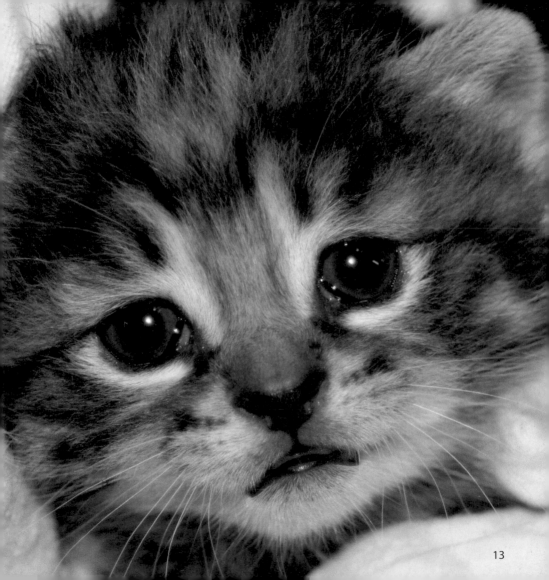

Species: Clouded Leopard

Name: Matsi

Home: Nashville Zoo at Grassmere, TN

Born: 5/2/2010

Status: Vulnerable

Christian Sperka

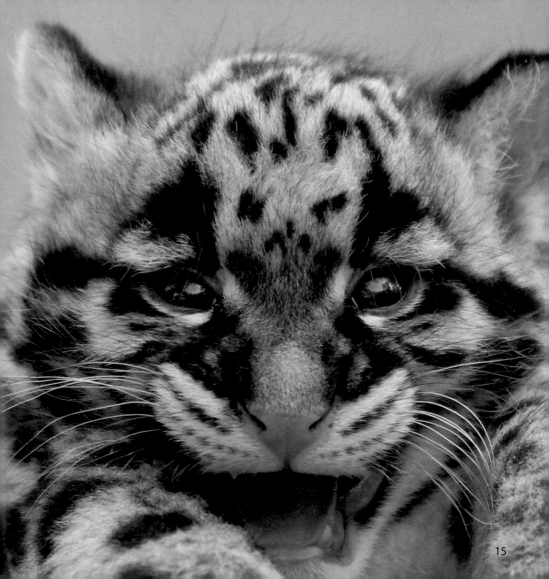

At one month old, little Matsi weighed just 1.5 lbs. One of only a few female cubs born in captivity, Matsi was the second birth for mom, Jing Jai, and dad, Arun.

Native to the dense forests of Southeast Asia, clouded leopards are considered the smallest of the large cats, weighing 30–50 pounds as adults. Clouded leopards' tails make up one-half of their five foot length. That long tail, combined with short legs and large paws, make clouded leopards well suited for treetop living.

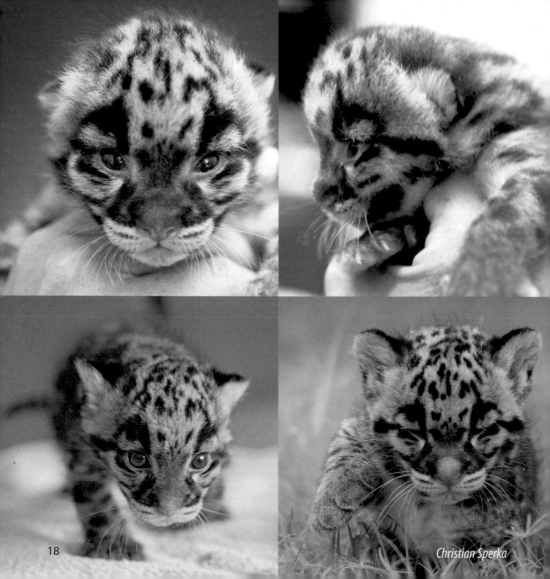

18

Christian Sperka

With deforestation, poaching, and capture for the pet trade on the rise, clouded leopards face serious threats to survival. Nashville Zoo participates in the Thailand Clouded Leopard Consortium, which leads a multifaceted conservation program that includes a viable self-sustaining breeding program.

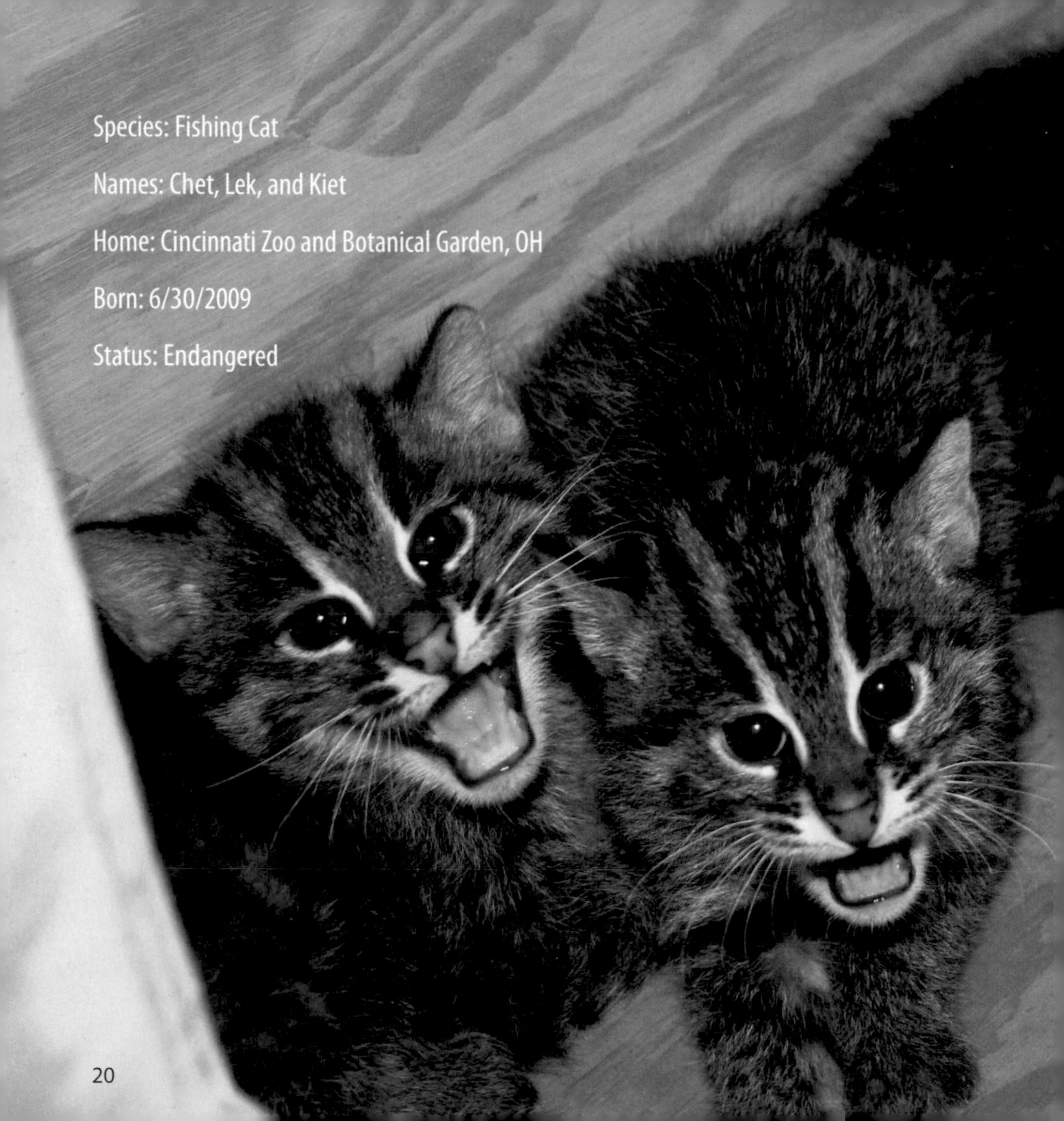

Species: Fishing Cat

Names: Chet, Lek, and Kiet

Home: Cincinnati Zoo and Botanical Garden, OH

Born: 6/30/2009

Status: Endangered

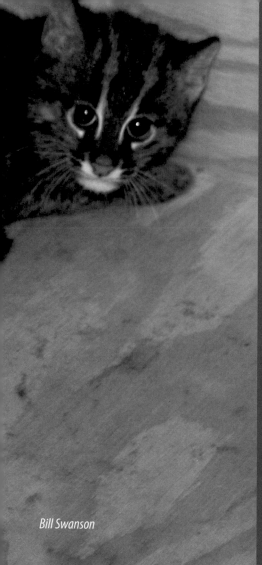

Bill Swanson

This lively trio of fishing cats is the first to be born at the Cincinnati Zoo in 15 years and the only litter born at an AZA-accredited institution in 2009 or 2010. Because the kittens' parents are descended from wild fishing cats in Thailand and Cambodia, these kittens are genetically valuable to the managed population.

Fishing cats are experts at seizing prey in the water. They'll plunge headfirst into a stream to nab a frog or even swim underwater to pursue a fish. Webbed toes help the cats maneuver in their aquatic habitat.

In 2003, the Cincinnati Zoo & Botanical Garden helped initiate the first comprehensive ecological study of wild fishing cats in Southeast Asia, an effort that continues today.

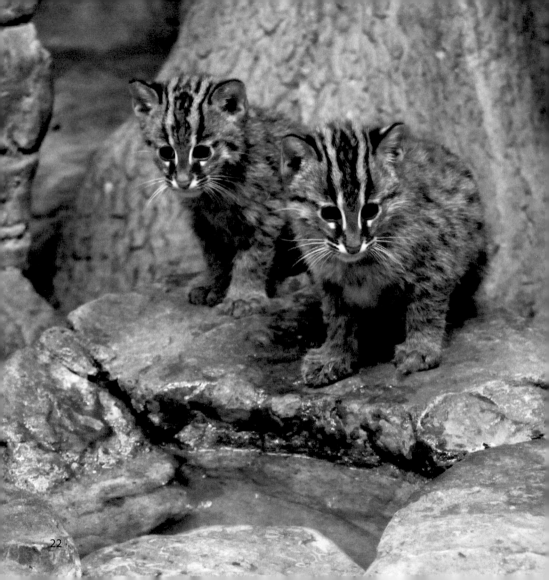

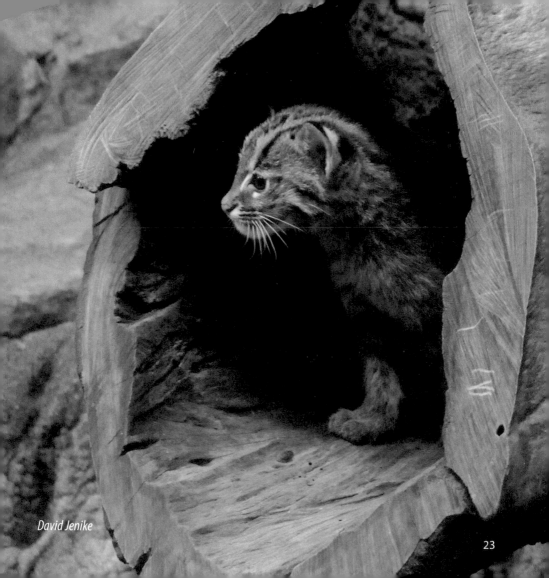

David Jenike

23

Species: Eurasian Lynx

Name: Blitz

Home: Nashville Zoo at Grassmere, TN

Born: 5/1/2010

Status: Least Concern

Christian Sperka

Born during a catastrophic storm that caused unprecedented flooding at Nashville Zoo and throughout the surrounding area, this tiny Eurasian lynx emerged healthy and strong.

With a larger range than any other cat, Eurasian lynxes prowl the forests of Europe, Central Asia, and Siberia. But because of their secretive nature, lynxes often go unnoticed by their human neighbors. Large feet, which act as snowshoes, and thick fur make this species particularly well-adapted to snowy winter weather.

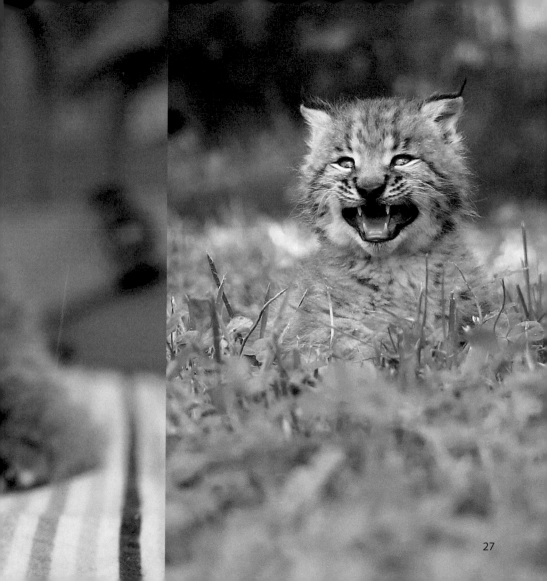

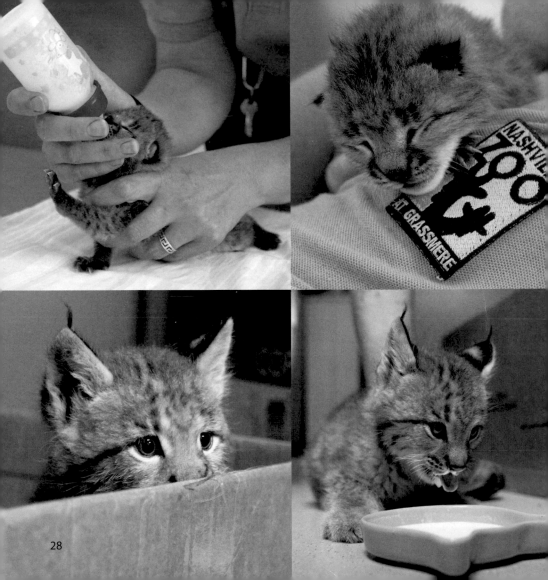

28

As part of Nashville Zoo's "Wildlife on Wheels" program, Blitz visits schools, senior centers, and hospitals, sharing his unique charm with those who may be unable to visit the zoo on their own.

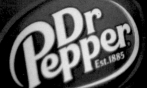

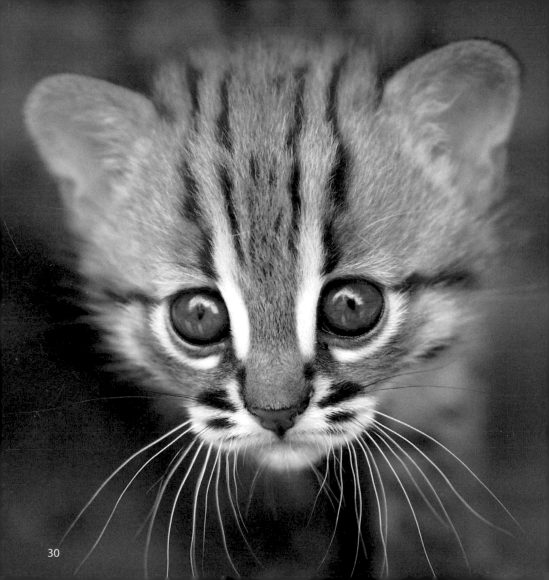

Species: Rusty-spotted Cat

Name: Yapahuwa

Home: Le Parc des Félins, France

Born: 4/25/2010

Status: Vulnerable

Papillon Usseglio

Rusty-spotted cats are the world's smallest feline species, followed closely by sand cats, black-footed cats, and oncillas. Well-adapted for climbing, these cats stalk birds, rodents, and reptiles in the trees and on the ground.

Little is known about this reclusive and nocturnal species, native only to India and Sri Lanka. Less than fifteen pictures of wild rusty-spotted cats have ever been published.

In 2001, Le Parc des Félins was the first French zoo to successfully breed rusty-spotted cats.

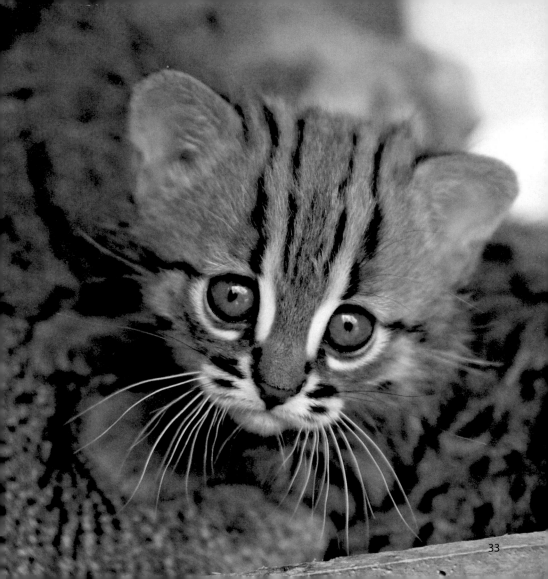
33

Species: Snow Leopard

Name: Laila

Home: Planckendael, Belgium

Born: 4/4/2010

Status: Endangered

Sander Hofman / Dirk Laenen (right) / Planckendael

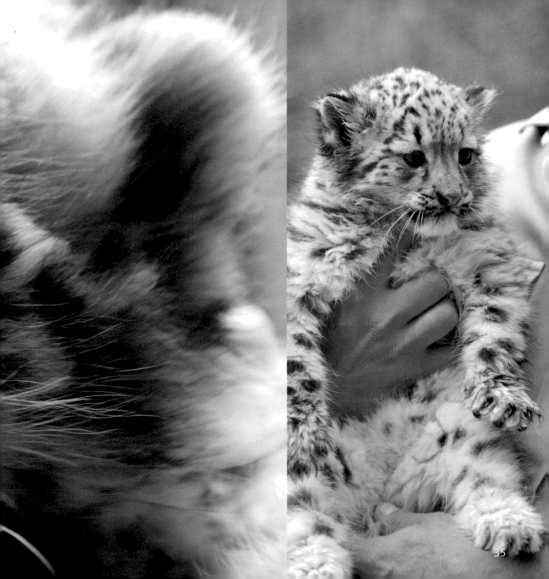

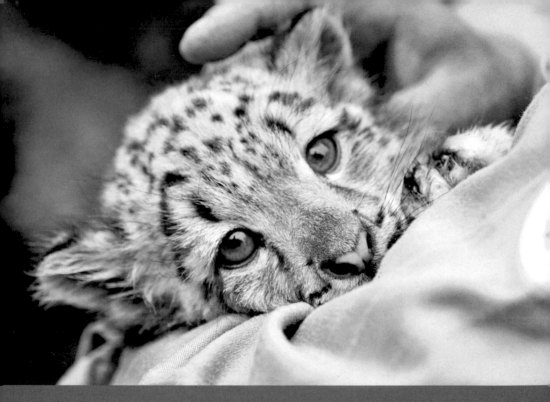

The first snow leopard to be born in Belgium, Laila had a difficult start in life. Shortly after Laila's birth, her mother's health declined rapidly, and, sadly, she did not survive. Planckendael keepers stepped in to raise the orphaned cub by hand. Now a healthy young adult, Laila represents an invaluable new bloodline for the European Snow Leopard Breeding Program.

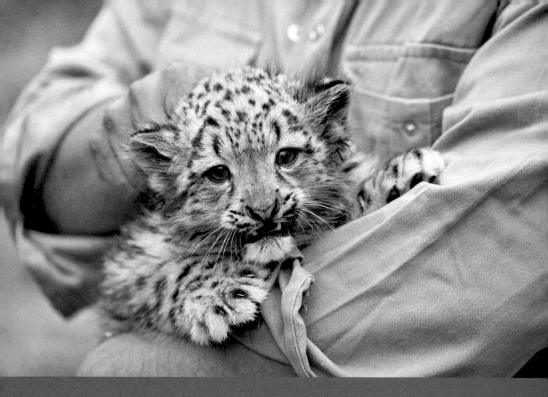

Snow leopards are exceptionally well-suited to life in the snow-covered mountains. Thick fur insulates them from the cold; small, stubby ears minimize heat loss; and wide, snowshoe-like paws feature furry undersides. Long flexible tails assist with balance as these dexterous cats hunt on treacherous rocky terrain. When sleeping, snow leopards use their long, fluffy tails like scarves to protect their faces from icy winds.

Dirk Laenen / Planckendael

Native to South and Central Asia, only 4,000 to 7,500 snow leopards may remain in the wild. Multiple agencies work to protect snow leopards, often focusing their efforts on offering economic alternatives to poaching for people living in snow leopard habitat.

These organizations create economic opportunities for local populations as a way to supplant poaching and reduce conflicts between snow leopards and herders.

Species: Sand Cat

Home: Al Ain Wildlife Park & Resort,
United Arab Emirates

Born: 5/24/2010

Status: Near Threatened

40

41

This litter marks the first successful sand cat births via in-vitro fertilization. The groundbreaking research behind this success was performed by Project Sand Cat, a collaborative effort between Al Ain Wildlife Park, the Cincinnati Zoo, and the University of Illinois.

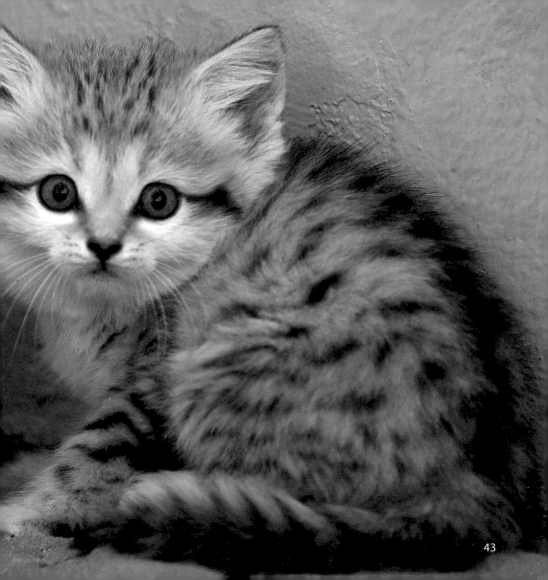

The smallest of the Arabian cats, sand cats are well adapted to the scorching days and frigid nights of their desert environment. Thick fur offers protection from the cold, while fluffy tufts between the toes insulate delicate paws from hot sand.

Venomous snakes like horned sand vipers are on the menu for these nocturnal hunters. Because sand cats get most of their moisture from their prey, they can venture far from water.

Al Ain's 34 sand cats represent the largest and most genetically significant captive population of sand cats at any single zoological institution.

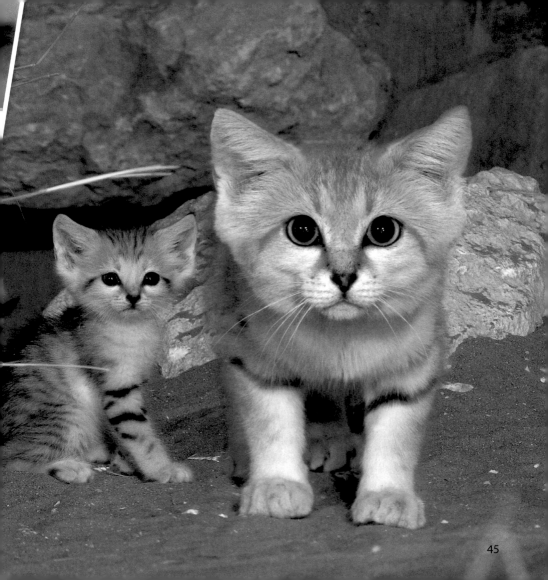

Species: Cheetah

Name: Kiburi

Home: San Diego Zoo Safari Park

Born: 11/14/2010

Status: Vulnerable

Of the 134 cheetahs born at the San Diego Zoo Safari Park, Kiburi is the first to be born to two hand-raised parents, Makena and Quint.

When Kiburi opened his eyes for the first time, he took in the world, gobbled a bottle of formula, played for a little while, and then fell fast asleep in front of the nursery's window. Weighing only 1.4 lbs. in most of these pictures, Kiburi's small size didn't stop him from frolicing with adorable ferociousness. At the nursery, Kiburi began "purring from day one," said Senior Nursery Keeper Sandy Craig.

Native to Africa, the Middle East, and India, cheetahs are the world's fastest land animal, reaching speeds up to 75 mph. Unlike most cats, cheetahs are poor climbers.

Zoological Society of San Diego

Kiburi means "proud" in Swahili.

48

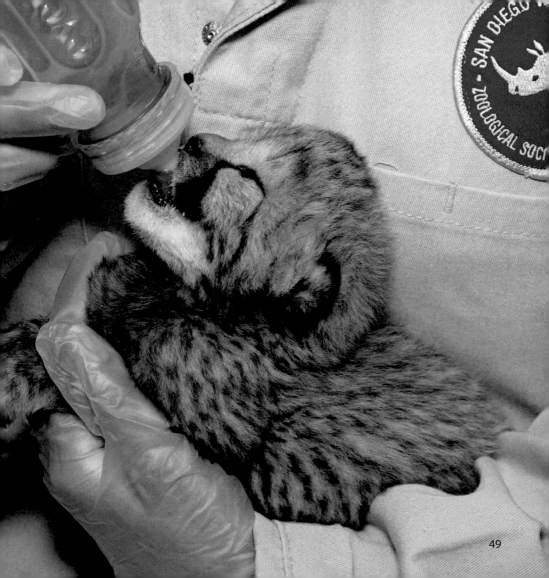

Cheetahs are important to Africa's growing ecotourism industry. As the local population learns that cheetahs attract tourist dollars, they are increasingly motivated to help protect these special animals.

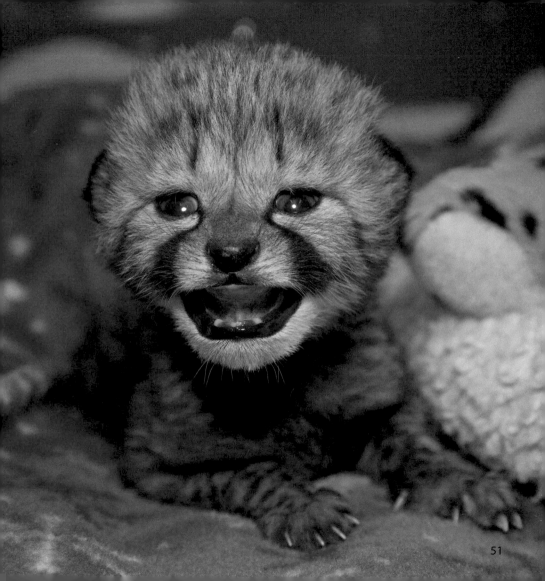

Species: Iriomote Cat

Name: Unnamed

Home: Iriomote Wildlife Conservation Center, Japan

Born: Unknown

Status: Critically Endangered

Among the rarest of all felines, only 100 Iriomote cats are estimated to live in the wild and all of these are confined to the remote Japanese island of Iriomote.

The Iriomote cat has a highly varied diet including reptiles, birds, insects, small mammals, and freshwater crustaceans but, above all, seems to enjoy dining on frogs!

Japan's Ministry of the Environment has worked hard to monitor and protect this critically endangered feline. Recent efforts to prevent interbreeding and disease from domestic and feral cats have proven successful. New efforts focus on preventing habitat destruction and reducing the threat of collisions with automobiles.

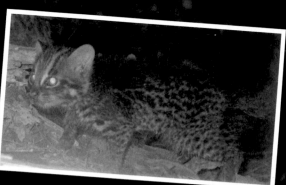

These may be the first photos of a juvenile Iriomote cat ever publishd.

Iriomote Wildlife Conservation Center

53

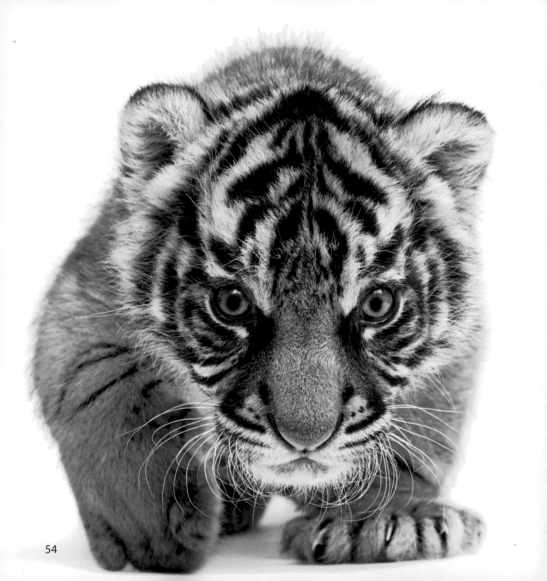

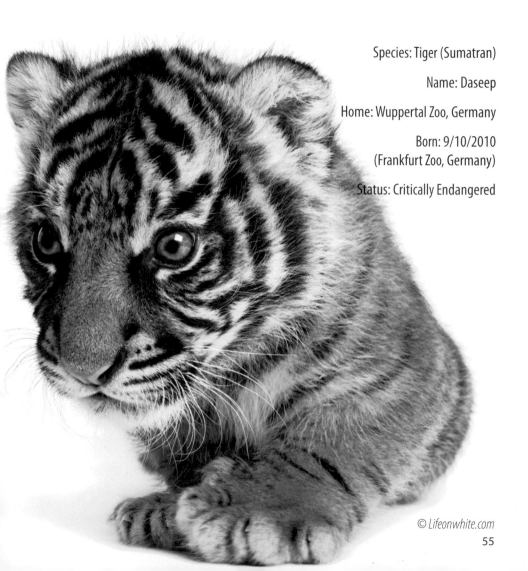

Species: Tiger (Sumatran)

Name: Daseep

Home: Wuppertal Zoo, Germany

Born: 9/10/2010
(Frankfurt Zoo, Germany)

Status: Critically Endangered

© Lifeonwhite.com

Native only to the Indonesian island of Sumatra, the Sumatran tiger is critically endangered with only 300–500 individuals remaining in the wild.

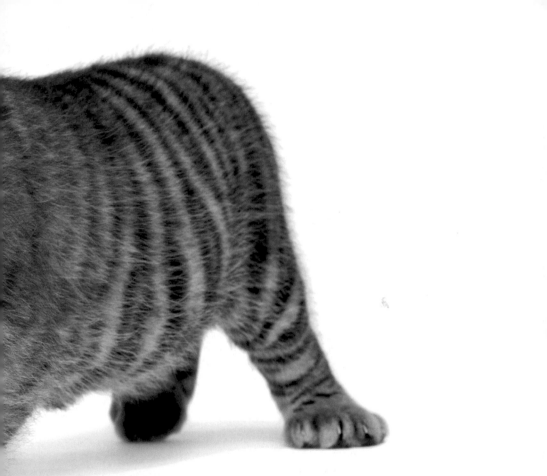

Poaching and deforestation from palm oil production threaten the Sumatran tigers' survival. In 2006 conservationists won a major victory with the establishment of the 400-square-mile Senepis Buluhala Tiger Sanctuary, yet the Sumatran tiger population continues to decline.

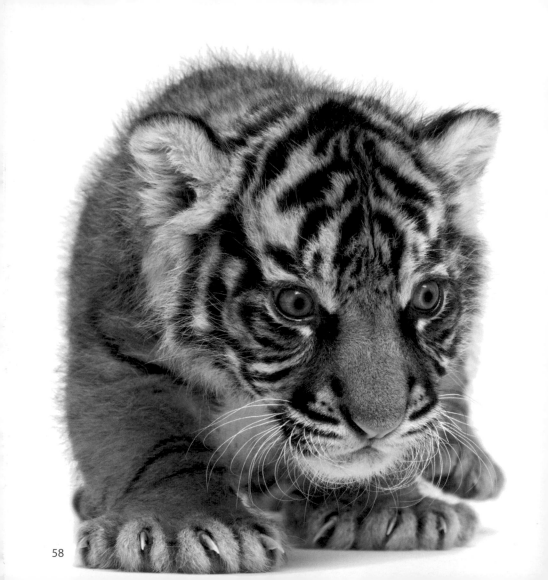

58

The smallest of all tigers, slender Sumatran tigers slip easily through dense rainforest vegetation.

Species: Serval

Names: Mischa & Unnamed Kitten

Home: Smithsonian National
Zoological Park, Washington, D.C.

Born: May 1991 & May 1992

Status: Least Concern

Servals' super hearing helps them locate prey in the tall grass of Africa's savannah. And when a bird flies low, watch out— servals can jump nine feet in the air to nab a feathery meal. Like all cats, servals learn survival skills from their mothers. Until kittens are ready to tag along on hunting trips, a cozy snuggle or free ride from mom will do just fine.

61

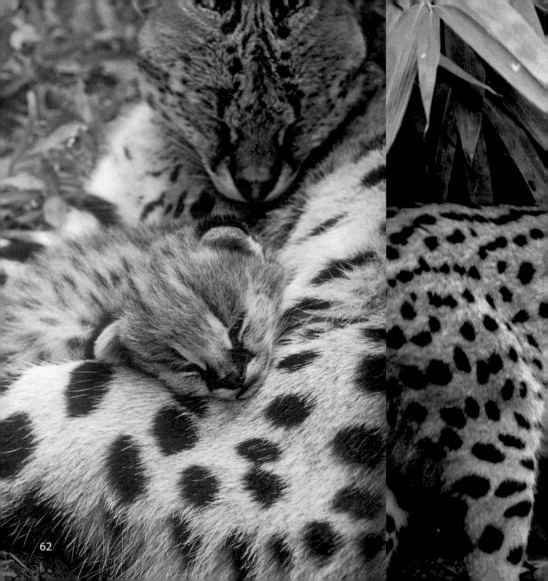

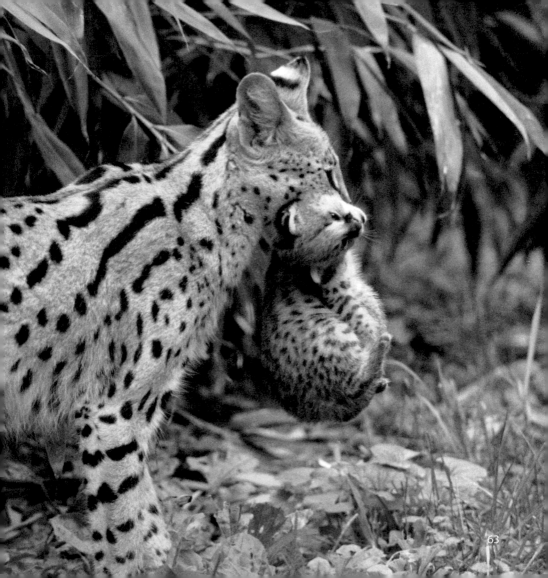

63

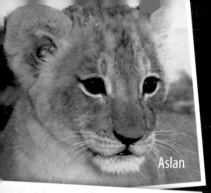

Aslan

Species: Lion (African)

Home: Smithsonian National Zoological Park, Washington, D.C.

Born: 8/31/2010 & 9/22/2010

Status: Vulnerable

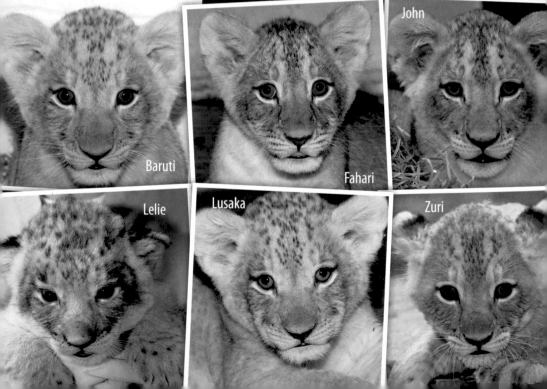

Baruti

Fahari

John

Lelie

Lusaka

Zuri

The Smithsonian National Zoological Park experienced a baby boom when lioness sisters Shera and Nababiep gave birth within just two weeks of one another to a combined seven cubs!

Building this impressive lion pride took years of planning, knowledge of the species' natural history, and familiarity with each lion's personality. Introducing Shera and Nababiep to Luke, the Zoo's adult male lion, began two years before the cubs' birth.

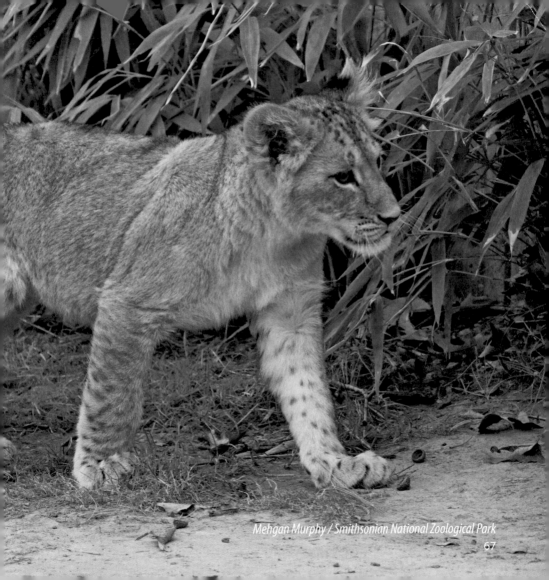

Because there is a large water feature in the main exhibit area, National Zoo keepers needed to administer a swim test before allowing the cubs to venture out on their own. Unlike tigers, which seem to enjoy a good swim, lions only reluctantly swim when they have to cross a small body of water.

Wild lion populations are rapidly vanishing due to habitat loss and conflicts with humans. While estimates vary, the species has seen a 30% to 50% population decline over the last two decades.

Species: Asiatic **Wildcat**

Home: Port Lympne Wild Animal Park, U.K.

Born: Unknown

Status: Least Concern

Neville Buck ©
70

New research suggests that our house cats are descended from Asian wildcats, which were first domesticated in the Near East around 8000 B.C. As humans stockpiled grains, which attracted rodents, the cunning kitties followed close behind looking for a tasty meal of their own. The wildcats were welcomed by farmers eager to keep pesky rodents away. The most significant threat to the Asiatic wildcat is interbreeding with domestic cats.

Species: Ocelot (Brazilian)

Name: Not Yet Named

Home: Connecticut's Beardsley Zoo

Born: 1/11/2011

Status: Endangered

73

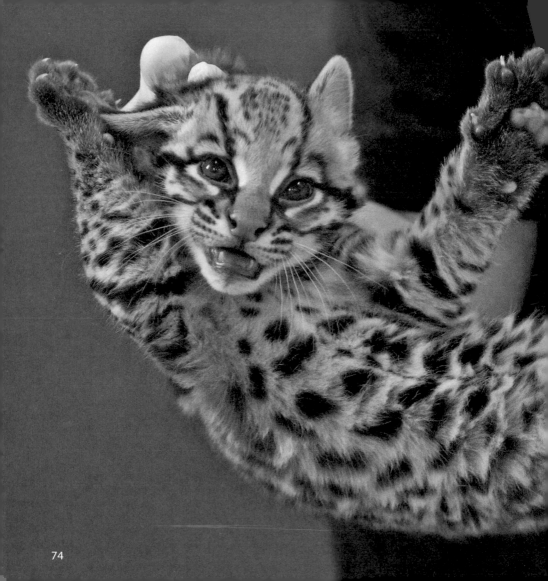

Weighing in at just three pounds in these photos, this three-month-old **ocelot kitten** was **the** product of groundbreaking reproductive science. Due to an injury, the kitten's mother, Kuma, was unable to breed naturally, making her a perfect candidate for new artificial insemination techniques pioneered by Connecticut's Beardsley Zoo and the Cincinnati Zoo's Lindner **Center** for Conservation & Research of Endangered Wildlife (CREW). This is the second kitten born **via** artificial insemination to Kuma.

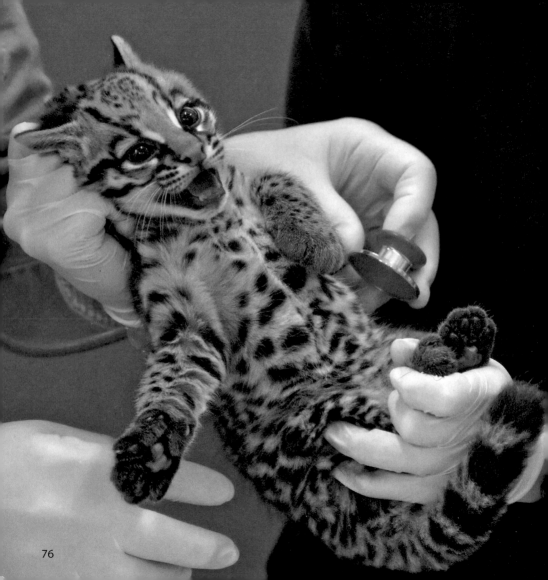

Like many of their small-sized feline relatives, Brazilian ocelots have been overlooked by scientists and conservationists. Very little is known about their behavior, reproduction, and population size.

Species: Pampas Cat

Names: Bopi

Home: Bioparque M'Bopicuá, Uruguay

Born: 2/7/2008

Status: Endangered

Small and heavy-bodied, South America's pampas cats are elusive and little-studied. Little "Bopi" was born at Uruguay's Bioparque M'Bopicuá, which works to protect and repopulate endangered native species. These efforts include environmental education programs that teach local schoolchildren to understand and appreciate the unique fauna of the region.

J.Villalba-Macias

Species: Margay

Names: Chokow Pol & K'o'ox

Home: Port Lympne Wild Animal Park, U.K.

Born: 4/4/2010

Status: Near Threatened

Living deep within South American rain forests, margays spend nearly all of their time in the trees. They are among the most dexterous of all cats and can rotate their ankles 180 degrees, allowing them to descend tree trunks head first and grasp branches with either front or hind paws!

Chokow and Ko'o'x were the first twin margays born in a European zoo.

Neville Buck ©

79

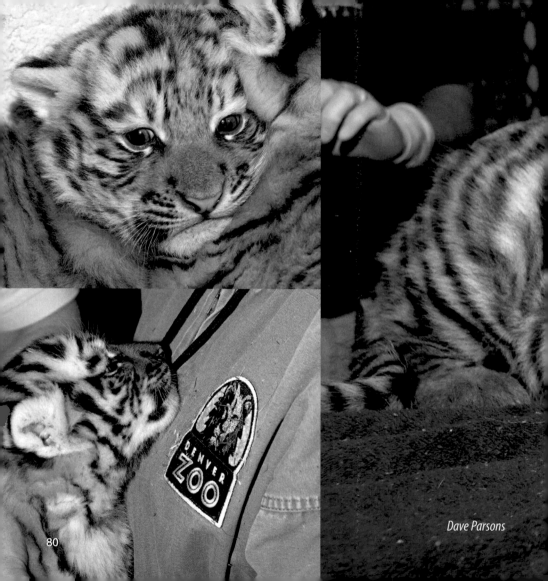

Dave Parsons

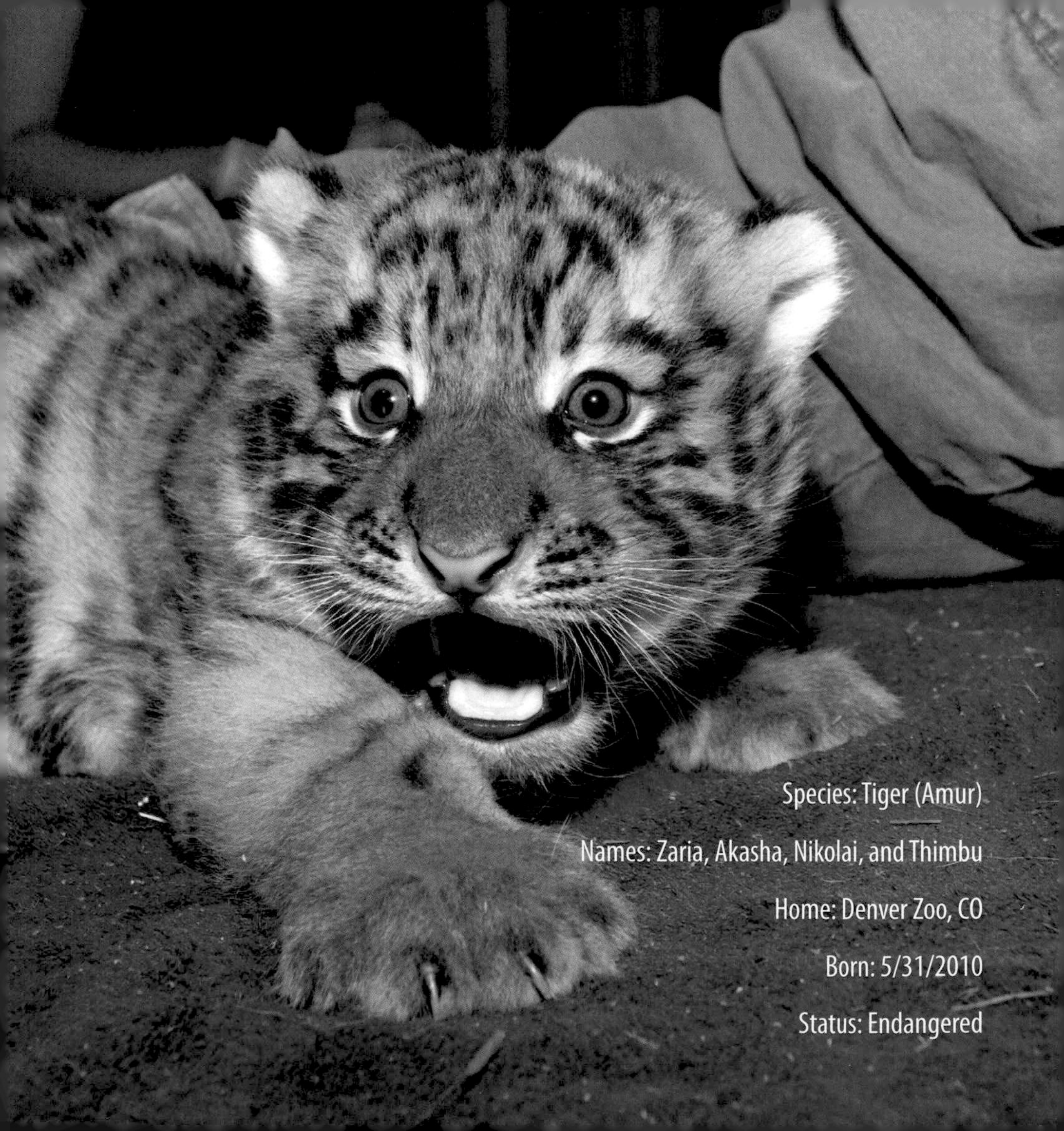

Species: Tiger (Amur)

Names: Zaria, Akasha, Nikolai, and Thimbu

Home: Denver Zoo, CO

Born: 5/31/2010

Status: Endangered

This pile of playful tiger cubs was born as part of the Association of Zoos and Aquariums' Species Survival Plan (SSP), which ensures healthy populations and genetic diversity among zoo animals.

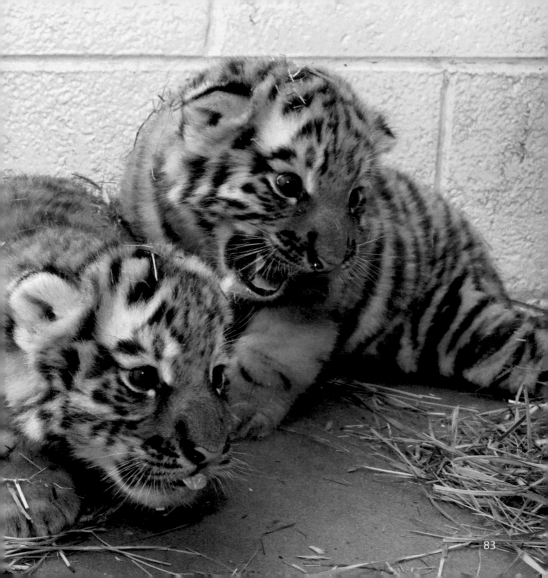

When full grown, these cubs will weigh up to 600 pounds and measure nine feet long.

Fewer than 400 Amur Tigers remain in the wild, where they are almost completely confined to the Amur River region of Asia's Far East. Though they are the largest of the six living tiger subspecies and the biggest of all wild cats, they are powerless against the effects of humans. In addition to habitat loss, Amur tigers face threats from poaching for their magnificent coat and for use of their body parts in traditional Chinese medicine.

Species: Guiña, Huiña, or Kodkod

Names: Kalki, Pikumche, and Tala

Home: Reserva Nacional de Fauna Andina Eduardo Avaroa, Bolivia

Born: Unknown

Status: Vulnerable

Fernando Vidal M, Fauna Andina Huiñas Project

The lifestyle and habits of these rare cats, found only in a narrow band of the Andes Mountains in Chile and Argentina, remain a mystery. These orphaned kittens were rescued by the Fauna Andina Huiñas Project, which aims to breed and release Guiñas back into the wild in Bolivia, where they once lived. These may be the only pictures of Guiña kittens ever published.

Antonio Rivas / Iberian Lynx Ex-situ Conservation Programme

Species: Iberian Lynx

Names: Espliego (this page), Elfo (opposite), Dalai & Dama (next page)

Home: Parque Nacional de Doñana, Spain

Born: 11/3/2008 (Elfo), 4/11/08 (Espliego), 3/23/07 (Dalai & Dama)

Status: Critically Endangered

89

With a total wild population of only 84–143 adults, the Iberian lynx hovers on the brink of extinction. Fortunately, researchers at Doñana National Park in Spain launched an ambitious breeding program to reintroduce these cats into the wild. Espliego, Elfo, Dalai, and Dama were all born and released as part of this effort.

The Iberian lynx sports shorter fur than other lynx species, making it better suited for the warm climates of Spain and Portugal.

Species: Asiatic Golden Cat

Name: Saigon

Home: Auckland Zoo, New Zealand

Born: 4/10/2005

Status: Near Threatened

Saigon is a rare treasure. While he was the only kitten born in his litter, this species is notoriously difficult to breed in captivity. When his mother proved a bit overzealous (she licked Saigon excessively!), zoo keepers hand-raised this special kitten.

Auckland Zoo

With a vocabulary that inlcudes purring, meowing, hissing, gurgling, growling, and spitting, Asiatic golden cats are one of the most vocal felines.

Species: Jungle Cat

Name: Nan

Home: Le Parc des Félins, France

Born: 3/3/2010

Status: Least Concern

When threatened, jungle cats let out a miniature roar and may even leap onto their would-be attackers.

Jungle cat mummies have been unearthed in Egyptian tombs, suggesting a close relationship with humans. Today jungle cats range from Egypt to India and as far south as Malaysia.

Joëlle Camus

Species: Pallas' Cat

Names: Igor, Boris, Viktor, Vera, & Sophia

Home: Cincinnati Zoo &
Botanical Garden, OH

Born: 5/10/2007

Status: Near Threatened

A domestic cat named Mouse foster-raised this entire litter of Pallas' cats while their birth mother was sick. After weaning from Mouse, Igor and siblings moved to the Zoo nursery until they could be introduced to their new homes.

Bill Swanson

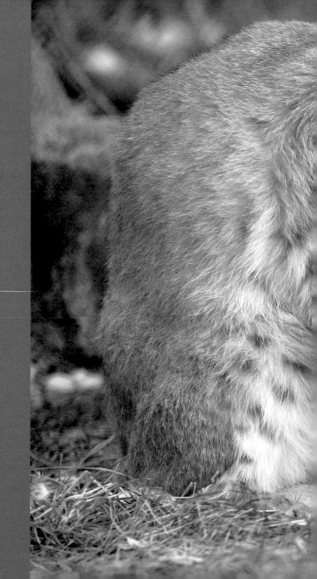

Species: Bobcat

Unnamed

Home: Assiniboine Park Zoo, Canada

Born: June 2005 and June 2006

Status: Least Concern

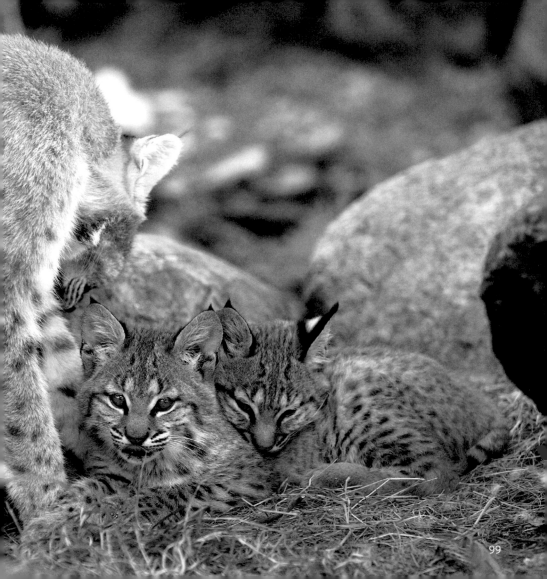

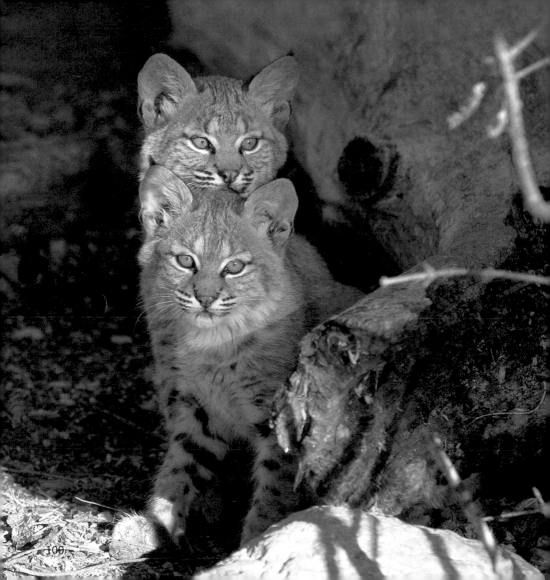

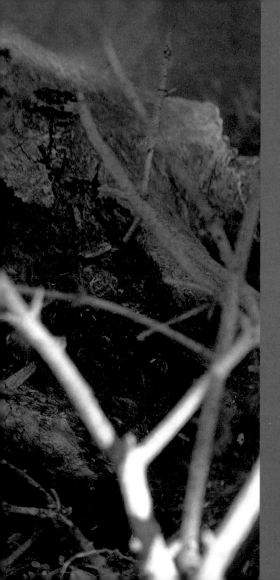

After taking a break at mom's side, the Assiniboine Park Zoo's pair of bobcat cubs is up for a game of hide and seek. Ranging over nearly all of the United States and Mexico, bobcats are shy and secretive in the wild. Bobcats' status, however, varies greatly from state to state: in some areas they are endangered, while in others, hunting of bobcats is permitted.

Weighing about 20–25 pounds, bobcats might be mistaken for large housecats except for their uniquely short or "bobbed" tail.

Species: Geoffroy's Cat

Name: Bart

Home: Dudley Zoo, U.K.

Born: 6/23/1994 (Banham Zoo, U.K.)

Status: Near Threatened

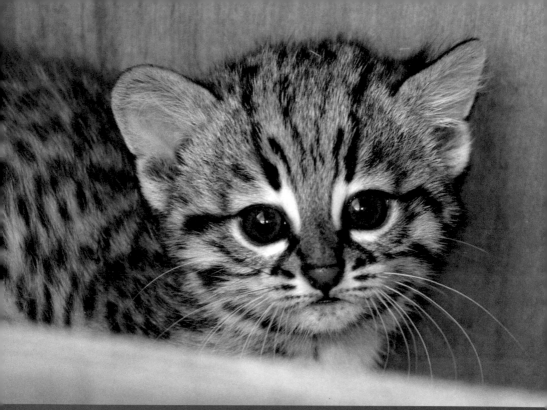

A particularly feisty chap, Bart came to Dudley Zoo as part of the European Species Survival Programme and has already fathered kittens of his own. Unlike most felines, Geoffroy's cats often stand upright on their hind legs to peer over the vegetation in their scrubby South American habitat.

Species: Cougar (North American)

Name: Palus

Home: Oregon Zoo, OR

Born: 9/19/2010

Status: Least Concern

Most cougar cubs are shy, but little Palus was described as "brave and feisty" by her keepers. Palus eagerly explored her new exhibit and quickly acclimated to her life in the spotlight. Like all cougars in accredited North American zoos, Palus' parents, Chinook and Paiute, were bred as part of the Association of Zoos and Aquariums' Puma Population Management Plan.

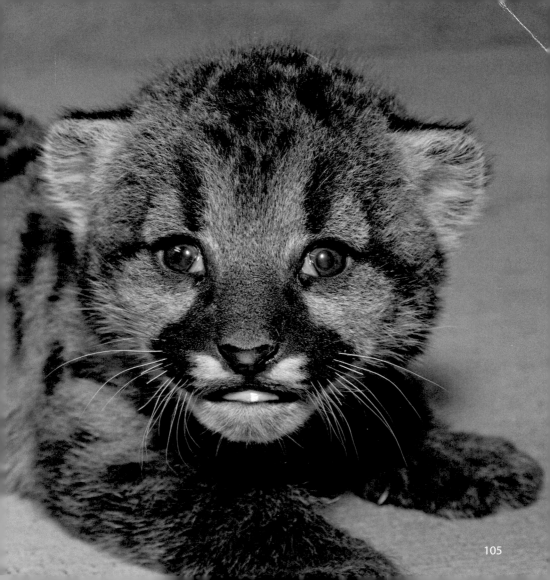

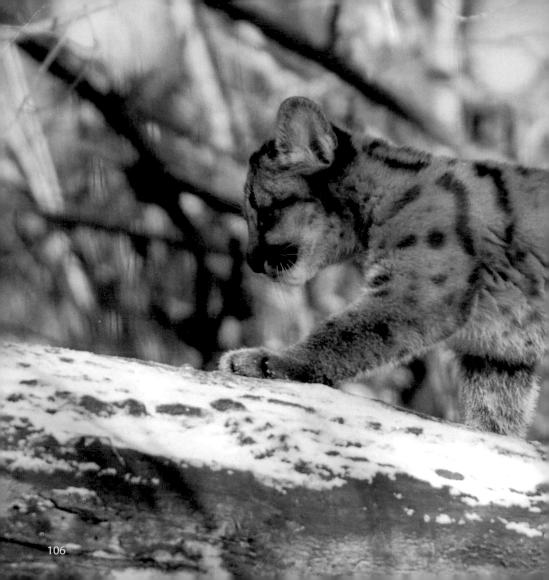

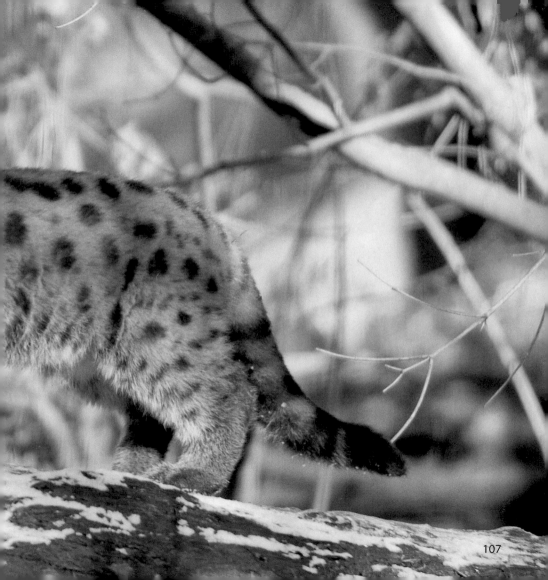

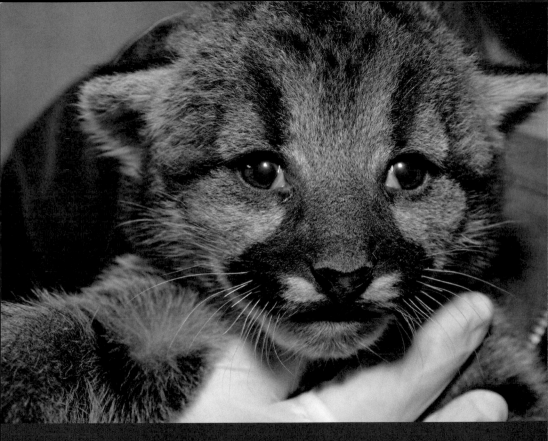

The cougar has the widest distribution of any land animal in North America, ranging from northern Canada to southern Argentina. Cougars are remarkably adaptable, inhabiting forests, deserts, mountains, and grasslands.

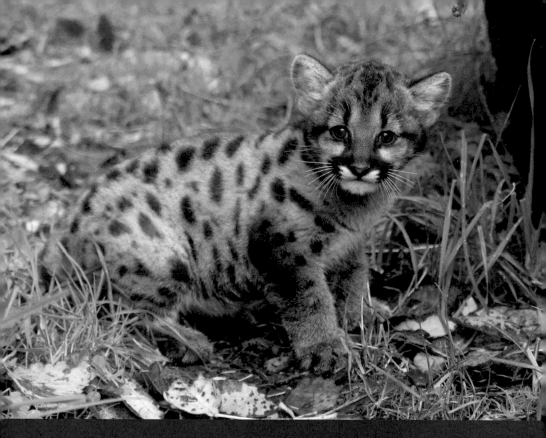

Exterminated in the eastern half of the United States during the early 1900s, the cougar is slowly making a comeback, most recently in Illinois and Michigan. As human recreation and development encroach on cougar habitat, conflicts are inevitable. Oregon Zoo's animal care staff has explored nonlethal methods, such as marking areas with tiger urine, to deter cougars from visiting campgrounds and neighborhoods

Species: Oncilla

Home: Fundación Botánica y Zoológica de Barranquilla, Colombia

Born: March 2010

Status: Vulnerable

Extra-large eyes help slender oncillas navigate the dark forests during nighttime prowls. Like many small cats, including its cousins, margays and ocelots, oncillas have not been well researched. Oncillas differ from their jungle-loving relatives in preferring cooler, high-altitude habitats.

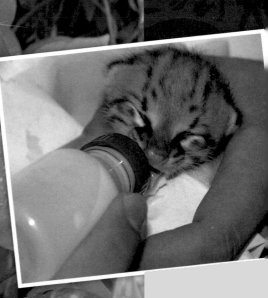

Fundación Botánica y Zoológica de Barranquilla

Species: Canada Lynx

Name: Bizhiw, Mary-Lou, & Timmy

Home: Assiniboine Park Zoo, Canada

Born: 6/4/2004 (Bizhiw)
5/23/2009 (Mary-Lou and Timmy)

Status: Least Concern

Darlene Stock

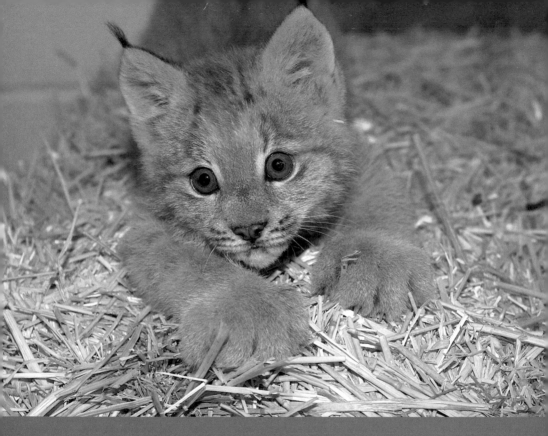

When a member of the Anishinabe aboriginal peoples found this tiny Canada lynx kit by the side of the road, the baby was taken in and nursed back to health. Named "Bizhiw," which is the Anishinabe name for lynx, the once-abandoned cat has now fathered four kittens of his own. One of Bizhiw's offspring was named Timmy in honor of the the Anishinabe elder who rescued Bizhiw.

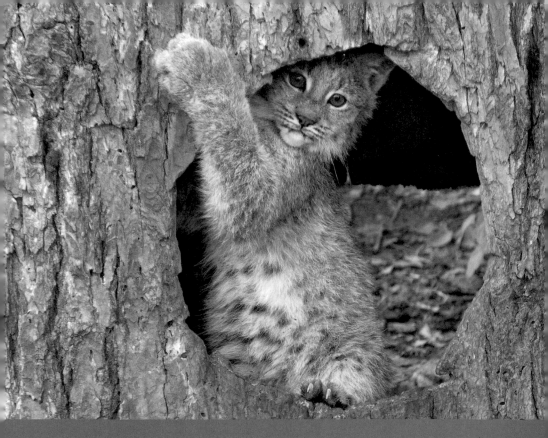

Canada lynx dine on a variety of birds and rodents but the snowshoe hare makes up the majority of its diet. Both predator and prey are uniquely suited for life in Canada's snowy wilderness.

Species: Jaguar

Name: Magala

Home: Bosphorus Zoo, Turkey

Born: 7/7/2008
ZooParc de Beauval, France

Status: Near Threatened

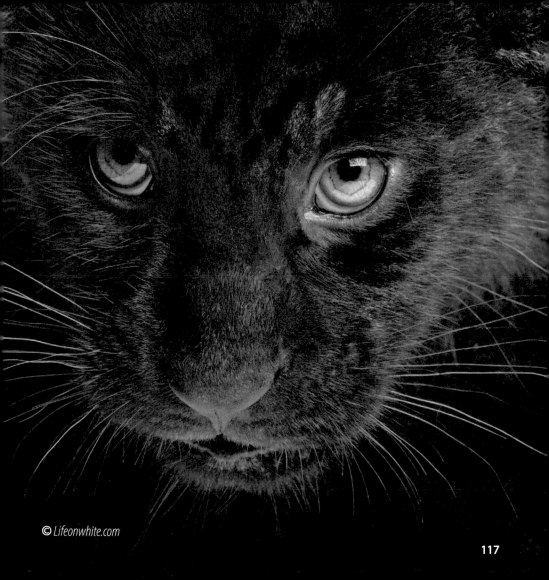

© Lifeonwhite.com

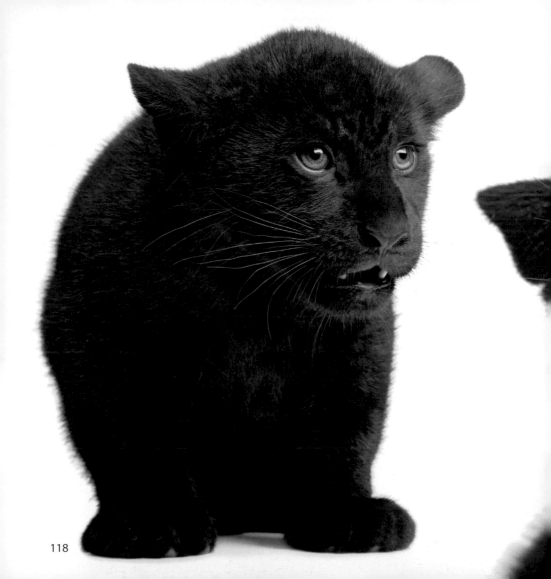

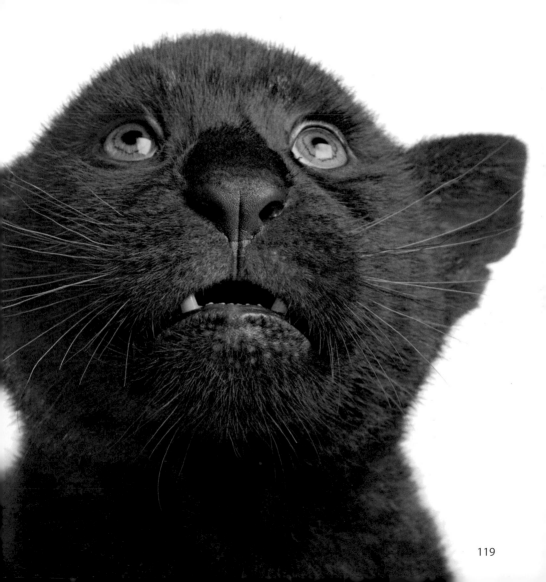

Jaguars are the only big cats native to the Americas and the third-largest cat species in the world (only lions and tigers are larger). As apex predators, jaguars hunt animals many times their size, including tapirs, cows, and horses. Extraordinarily powerful jaws enable jaguars to pierce the shells of armored prey such as turtles and armadillos.

About 6% of jaguars exhibit high levels of dark pigmentation, a trait called melanism. This harmless condition results in an all-black appearance as demonstrated by little Magala. Melanistic jaguars are called black panthers and may be mistaken for a separate species, but they are in fact the same species as jaguars with spotted coats.

Habitat destruction, poaching, and conflict with ranchers have led to a rapid decline in jaguar populations. Groups like the Jaguar Conservation Fund focus on protecting the habitats of both jaguars and their prey species while reducing human-jaguar conflict.

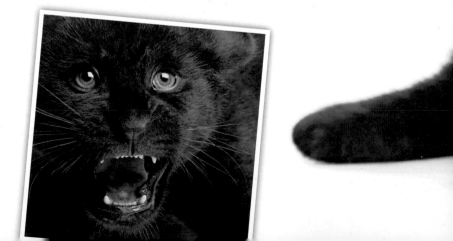

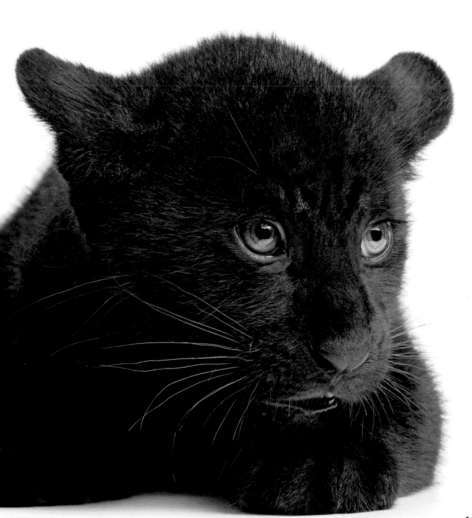

Species: Jaguarundi

Names: Aguapo

Home: Le Parc des Félins, France

Born: 11/18/2009

Status: Least Concern

Joëlle Camus

With reddish brown fur, short legs, and a long body, jaguarundis are often mistaken for otters or martens! While most small Central and South American felines are nocturnal, jaguarundis hunt, explore, and play by day, making them popular with zoo visitors.

In 2008, Le Parc des Félins was the first European zoo to breed jaguarundis and now coordinates breeding efforts for this species on behalf of the European Species Survival Programme.

Species: Caracal

Names: Indra and Iniko

Home: Olmense Zoo, Belgium

Born: 4/4/2008

Status: Least Concern

Even as kittens, caracals exhibit the black-tipped ears characteristic of the species. In fact, the word "caracal" comes from a Turkish word meaning "black ear." Caracals' tufted ears help them locate prey.

Caracals are exceptional hunters across a wide variety of terrain. Stiff hairs between the caracal's paws allow them to move swiftly across loose sand while excellent climbing abilities help them hunt tasty but ever-vigilant hyraxes. Caracals are even outstanding midair hunters, leaping vertically to catch birds out of the sky, sometimes snagging two at a time!

Olmense Zoo

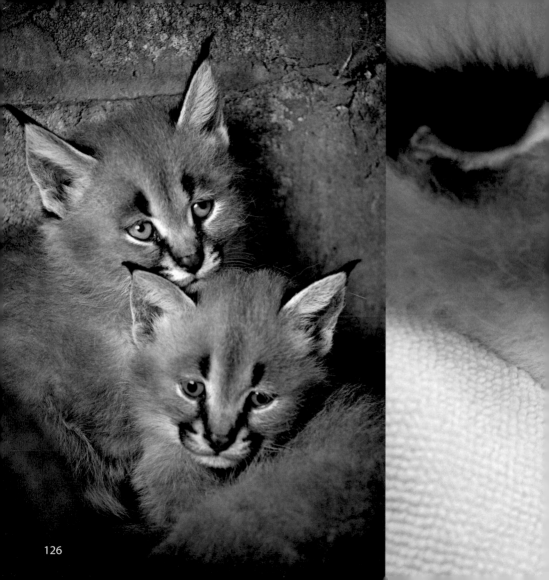

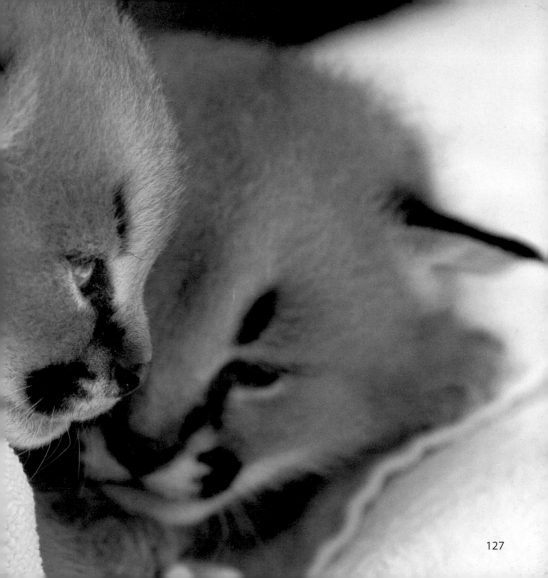

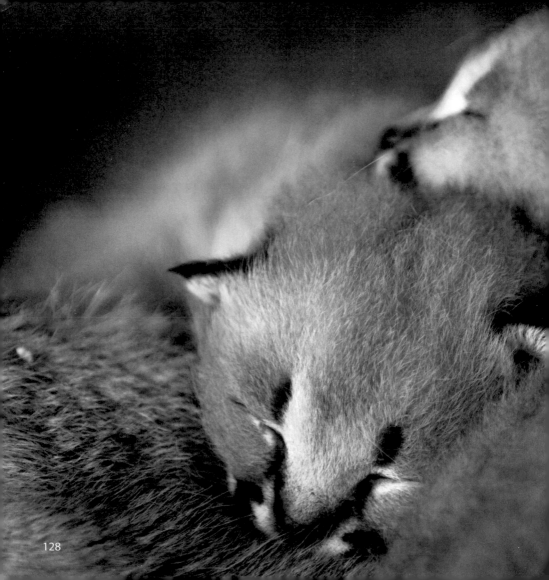

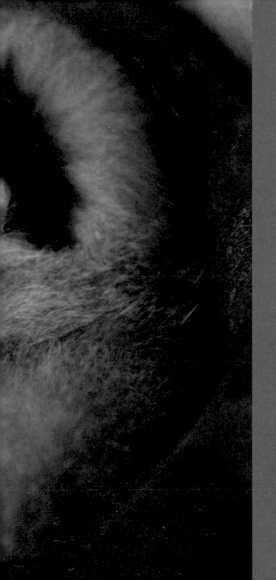

Inhabiting the dry steppes, savannahs, and scrub forests of Africa and the Middle East, caracals are rarely seen despite their robust numbers.

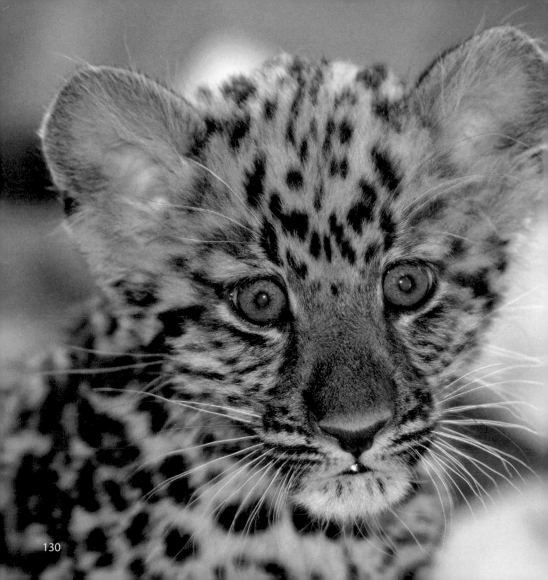

Species: Leopard (Amur)

Name: Tuffy

Home: Jacksonville Zoo & Gardens, FL

Born: 8/27/2010

Status: Critically Endangered

John Reed Photography

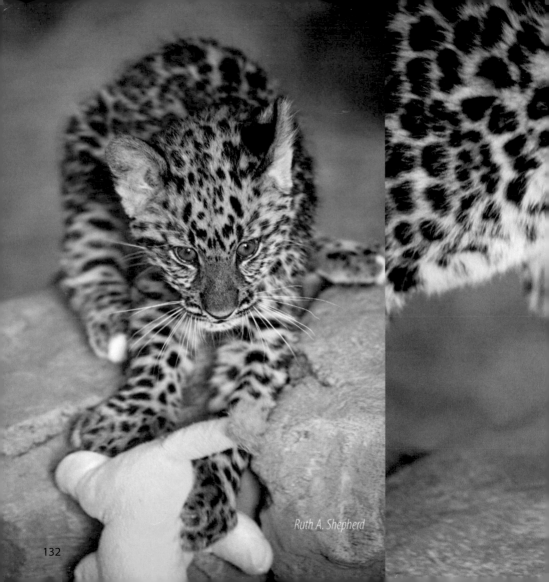

Ruth A. Shepherd

132

With only 30–35 individuals remaining in the wild, Amur leopard are among the world's rarest and most endangered felines. To protect these exquisite animals, The Amur Leopards and Tiger Alliance developed a comprehensive conservation program focused on deterring poaching, educating native peoples, and studying wild leopards.

The Amur leopard's remaining range straddles remote mountains between Russia, China, and Korea, complicating conservation efforts.

"The Jacksonville Zoo and Gardens participates in many important conservation programs. But rarely do we get a chance to make a contribution to such a critical program," explained Jacksonville Zoo and Gardens' Executive Director Tony Vecchio. "The Amur leopard is so close to the brink of extinction that every birth is significant."

Ruth A. Shepherd

Species: Lion (Asiatic)

Names: Jasraj & Jeevana

Home: Zürich Zoo, Switzerland

Born: 2/3/2009

Status: Endangered

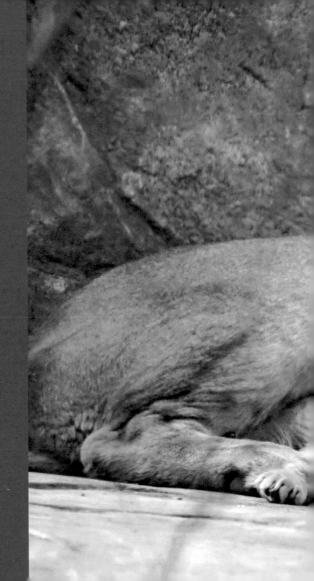

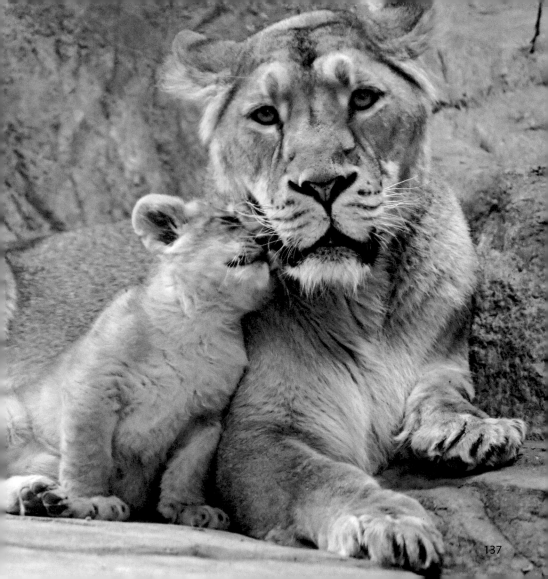

Once ranging from Italy and Greece through India and Iran, today the Asiatic lion population is mostly confined to the small Gir Forest National Park and Wildlife Sanctuary in India.

Urgent efforts are underway to protect the few hundred wild lions remaining, including involving local villagers in conservation projects. Zoo babies, like Jasraj and Jeevana, offer hope for the survival of this rare cat.

Asiatic lions are highly social like their African cousins, but males tend to interact less with the pride. This may be due to the fact that prey species tend to be smaller in Asia, requiring fewer lions to take down dinner.

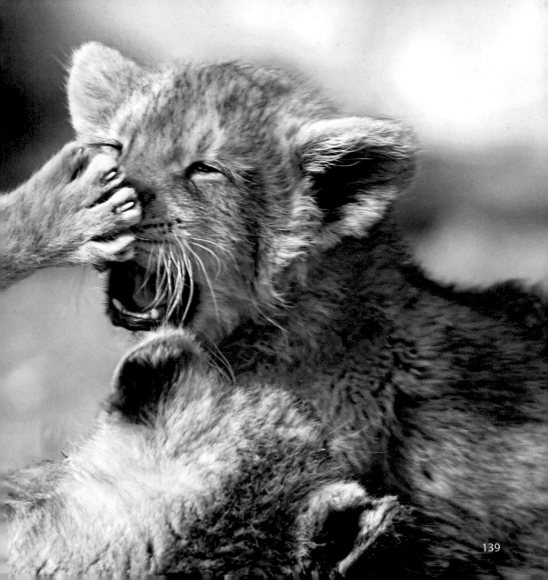

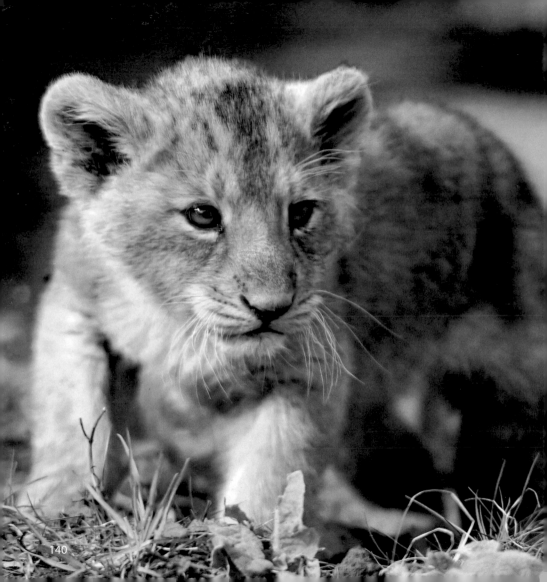

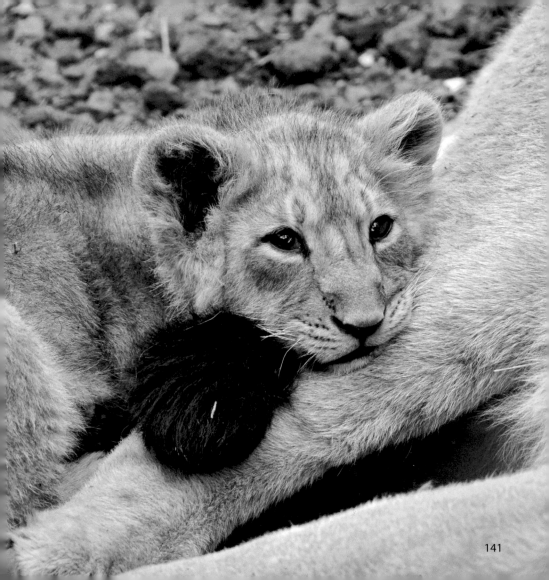

Acknowledgments

Thanks to the institutions and organizations that made *ZooBorns Cats!* possible:

Amur Leopard and Tiger Alliance

Assiniboine Park Zoo

Association of Zoos and Aquariums

Auckland Zoo

Belfast Zoo

Belize Zoo

Bioparque M'Bopicuá

Bronx Zoo

Burgers Zoo

Canadian Association of Zoos and Aquariums

Cincinnati Zoo and Botanical Garden

Connecticut's Beardsley Zoo

Denver Zoo

Dudley Zoo

Ex-situ Conservation Program - Parque Nacional de Doñana

Felid TAG

Fort Worth Zoo

Fresno Chaffee Zoo

Fundación Botánica y Zoológica de Barranquilla

Fundación Botánica y Zoológica de Barranquilla

Henson Robinson Zoo

Hogle Zoo

Houston Zoo

International Society for Endangered Cats (ISEC) Canada

Iriomote Wildlife Conservation Center

Kansas City Zoological Park

Le Parc des Félins

Life on White

Linton Zoo

Nashville Zoo at Grassmere

Olmense Zoo

Oregon Zoo

Planckendael

Port Lympne Wild Animal Park

Reserva Nacional de Fauna Andina Eduardo Avaroa

San Diego Zoo Safari Park

San Francisco Zoo

Smithsonian National Zoological Park

Snow Leopard Trust

University of Oxford, Department of Zoology

Utah's Hogle Zoo

Wildlife Conservation Society, Lao Peoples Democratic Republic Office

Wuppertal Zoo

Zoo Costa Rica

Zoo Heidelberg

Zoo Melaka Malaysia

Zoo Negara Malaysia

Zoo Sauvage de Saint-Félicien

ZooParc de Beauval

INDEX OF ANIMALS

INDEX OF ZOOS

About the Authors

Andrew Bleiman spends his days working in new media strategy and nights dreaming of ways to spend more time at zoos and aquariums. He graduated from the University of Pennsylvania with a degree in English literature and a yet to be recognized minor in baby animal-ology. Andrew lives in Chicago, Illinois, with his wife, Lillian, and their dogs, Izzy and Mathman.

Chris Eastland is a classically trained portrait artist and a freelance web and graphic designer. While Chris loves all the ZooBorns, he's particularly partial to primates and cats. He lives in Brooklyn with his cat Georgie.

Andrew and Chris share a passion for connecting people and animals, and with ZooBorns they hope to raise awareness of the vital role zoos and aquariums play in conservation. To learn more about the animals in this book—and to meet even more zoo babies—visit their website, ZooBorns.com.